Cuz I Like Me

Kim Artis Jones

DEDICATION

Dedicated to my Mom, Ozabelle Jones. You always listened to my poems, and asked, "Where did you get those words?" I'd answer, 'They're in my head." I've now put them in this book for others to enjoy.

Contents

ACKNOWLEDGMENTS

Ah, where do I start? This book is just a glimpse of me and the "madness that is in my head". I'd like to thank my family for putting up with me spouting words of rhyme. My editor, Donna Knutson for every period, comma, tense change and pushing me to birth this book. Waymon Harrold for the cover design, YOU Nailed IT!!!.

There are Assets & Liabilities in the Balance Sheet of Life.

~~*Artis*~~

Ozabelle

Ozabelle McCray Jones

*O*mnipotent
*Z*ealous
*A*mazing
*B*eautiful
*E*mpathetic
*L*oving
*L*oyal
*E*legant

*M*other
*C*aring
*C*reative
*R*adiant
*A*doring
*Y*outhful

*J*oyous
*O*utspoken
*N*oble
*E*mpowering
*S*tylish

HER LIFETIME

9 decades

3 years

5 months

10 days

The day she was born,

Herbert Hoover was president.

Witnessed 16 presidents, 24 elections

Great Depression

WW II

Atomic bomb

Montgomery Boycotts

Civil Rights Movement

Vietnam War

Apollo 13 Space Mission

Watergate

Challenger Disaster

Reaganomics

Gulf War

Release of Nelson Mandela

September 11

Hurricane Katrina

Invasion of Iraq

Election of a Black President

Rise and fall of ISIS

Killing of Osama bin Laden

Legalization of Same Sex marriage

#MeToo, women fight back

Black Lives Matter Movement

COVID-19 Pandemic

1st Black Woman VP and Presidential Nominee

The invention of:

Polio Vaccine

Hula Hoop

Color TV

Miniskirt

go-go Boots

Bell Bottoms

Platform Shoes

Prime Time Soaps

Rubik's Cube

CD Player

Sony Walkman

The Internet

Digital Cameras

Hip Hop

Cell phones

Instagram

Facebook

Smart watches

Boxed mattresses

Drones

Selfie Sticks

Artificial Intelligence

93 years

9 decades

3 years

5 months

10 days

WHAT MAMA DID

What Mama did, she did out of love,
Seeking direction from above.
What Mama did, she thought was right,
Believing it would make your future bright.
What Mama did, was what she knew,
Hoping that faith would bring her through.
Mama didn't have an action plan.
Her motive was to withstand,
The roaring storms that came her way.
Would not deter or cause her to stray.
What Mama did, she did to survive,
Encouraged you to persevere and strive.
What Mama did, was her very best,
Through trial and error, she passed life's test.
What Mama did, was settle the score,
Instilled confidence and allowed you to soar.
She did what she had to do...
To produce a better her, in you!

Positively Me

DARE

From the moment it is created in one's mind,
A thought with action can change mankind.
It can result in an antidote for a disease.
It can enable people to live a life of ease.
Give the downtrodden hope,
Allow the disenchanted to cope.
Dare to dream, dare to inspire,
Ignite a passionate fire.
Keep the dream alive.

CAN I COME??

Can I come, or can I join in?
Release words through paper and pen.

Can I come divulge my soul?
Allow my thoughts to unfold.
Can I come release my stress?
Get some things off my chest.

Can I come give another perspective,
Dissolve the negative?
Can I come ease the load?
Lead you down a different road.

Can I come enlighten your spirit,
Entice you to relax a bit?
Can I come, help you unwind?
Emancipate your mind.

Can I come introduce some fun?
Humor you with a slick tongue.
Can I come offer my assistance?
Remove any thoughts of resistance.

Can I come…
Raise you up,
Fill your cup,
Wash away the grime,
Get some of your time,
Let you experiment,
Alter your temperament,
Make a fresh start,
Heal your broken heart.

Can I come? Will you allow me in?
Soothe you with my paper and pen.

A PEACE OF ME

The words I write come from deep within my soul.
Sometimes they run hot, other times dripping cold.
They can be soft and fluffy, like a cloud
Or bright, vibrant, and loud.

Scenarios unfold in my head,
So to the pen and paper, I am led.
As the curtain begins to rise,
Euphoria appears before my eyes.

Serenity and calmness envelope my being.
As the pen writes what my heart is seeing,
An orgasmic flow of thoughts to words.
Words that allow my thoughts to be heard.

Surreptitiously, my soul is revealed,
Secrets of my spirit no longer concealed.
Writing unleashes the ability
To release a "peace" of me.

I'M FLYING SOLO

I'm flying solo.
Spreading my wings, watch me glow.
No longer concerned about what people think.
No longer searching for that link.
Don't need anyone riding shotgun.
Those days are over and done.

Not waiting around for someone to tag along.
Stepping to the mic and singing my own song.
Taking a walk on the wild side.
Letting my hair down, rolling back the top,
And enjoying the ride.

I'm going to do all the things I want to,
Even things that are sometimes done by two.
Take that vacation trip.
Go to the islands on a cruise ship.
Try out that place to eat.
Walk right on in and take a seat.
Check out a show or movie.
Go to the museum and even sightsee.
Cuz, I only have to answer to me.

Won't let life pass me by,
Gonna live life to the fullest until I die.
Bags packed, car gassed up and ready to go.
I'll catch you next time, but right now...
I'm flying solo!

BLACK COFFEE

Hot
Strong
Freshly Brewed
Rich
Savory
Tasty
No Sugar
No Cream
Black
Coffee
Would you Like a CUP?

CHOCOLATE DROP

Never really liked this term
When I was young.
Thought it was derogatory
Aimed at my complexion.

As I matured,
Watched society
Envy
This hue I be.

Most of their time
Spent on the beach
Desperately trying to reach
This skin tone
In which I was born.

Like chocolate
There are many hues
From which to choose—
Creamy, milky, café au lait, caramel, cocoa, dark.

Smooth or silky,
Bold or rich,
Bitter or sweet,
They're all unique.

Today,
Grown and sexy,
Cream of the crop,
So, give me my props.
Call me…
CHOCOLATE DROP!!!

MY RIGHT

I've been told I'm picky, is that not my right?
To want enhancement and assurance that I shine bright.
Surrounding myself with positivity is not an egotistical plight;
It is validation of a safe and secure flight.

I want to enjoy and live my life,
Free from drama and strife.
Minor idiosyncrasies are so trite,
And will only hinder my flight.

It is my right to be discerning,
To find the serenity my soul is yearning.
Every day brings facets of learning,
Keep my thoughts internally burning.

When I say someone or something is not for me,
I'm not claiming superiority,
I'm proclaiming my right of individuality,
The right to be and think freely.

I will struggle with all power and might
And never surrender without a fight.
The sanctity of my soul always in sight,
Because being selective is my God-given right.

Happily Ever After

Someone stole my happily ever after.
Loaded everything in a 16-wheel tractor.
I'm not talking about my knight in shining armor,
Or things found in fairytale folklore.
No, I got jacked for so much more.

As I stand here,
Some things aren't real clear.
I can't be sure,
I think I opened the door.

First came in doubt.
I thought I knew what she was all about.
She crept in
With the "you can't win" spin.

Next came insecurity.
Giving doubt validity.
She piggybacked
And emphasized all I lacked.

Then, worry showed up in a hurry
With a bunch of insecure and scary stuff
As to why, I wasn't good enough.

These three, on a mission
To send me deep into depression,
To crush my dreams,
Destroy my self-esteem.

But when I began to rewind
All these things in my mind,
I knew they weren't right.
Saw a glimmer of light.
Pulled myself out of that place.
Wiped the tears from my face.
Knew I had a choice.
Chose to listen to my inner voice.

I had been deceived.
Drawn away from what I believed---
A total essence.
Confidence, security and assurance.
I let doubt, insecurity and worry
Make my outlook blurry.
These three pegged me wrong.
Didn't realize I was really strong.
Thought they could bring me down.
But the inner me was sound.

Confidence assured me happily ever after
Was not in that tractor.
Disputing what they said
Victory was in my heart and in my head.
Fear should not be perceived.
Faith in what I believed.
My mindset, the determining factor
Of my happily ever after.

UNDERESTIMATED

Underestimated my skills
Because my talents were not revealed.
Underestimated my intelligence
Because my spirit was not plagued by vengeance.

Underestimated my abilities
Because my persona emitted serenity.
Underestimated my integrity
Because my emotions were held in secrecy.
Underestimated my worth
Because of the color in which I was birthed.

Your assumptions have made you blind.
Society has labeled my kind.
Therefore, I've been put in a bind.
Constantly striving to change your mind.
Always having to prove myself.
To reassure you, I'm not like anyone else.

Complicated
Liberated
Emancipated
Sophisticated
Educated,
But still,
Underestimated!!

IT JUST MAY BE

It just may be that I'm
Too critical
Or too cynical,
Too loud
Or too proud,
Too black
Or possess something you lack.

It just may be that I'm
Too choosy
Or too bluesy,
Too revealing
Or too feeling,
Too tall
Or you think that I have it all.

It just may be that I'm
Too keen
Or too mean.
Too picky
Or too sticky.
Too cold
Or just too damn bold.

It just may be that I'm
Too easy
Or too pleasing.
Too funny
Or too sunny.
Too complicated
Or more than you anticipated.

It just may be that I'm
Too bad
Or too mad.
Too happy
Or too sappy.
Too good
Or think more of myself than I should.

Or......It just may be.... Me!

I WILL NOT APOLOGIZE

I WILL NOT apologize for being me
Outspoken
Intelligent
Proud
Confident
Strong
And
Even defiant

I WILL NOT apologize for how I think
Positive
Independent
Egotistical
Critical
Analytical
And
Yes, superior

I WILL NOT apologize for how I look
Sexy
Sultry
Tall
Voluptuous
Shapely
In
Cocoa brown skin

The product of a divine entity.
The definition of who I am,
A sandwich of peanut butter and jam

An apology, I WILL NEVER make
Because that would mean God made a mistake!

CUZ I LIKE ME

First, let me explain
Under no circumstances am I vain.
When you see me walking by
Tall, straight and my head held high
I'm not being uppity,
Or claiming superiority.
It's just that I'm happy; you see
I'm happy, cuz I like me.

I've taken a different outlook,
A positive point of view, that's my nook.
Why would I be miserable?
How is that valuable?
Life is too short to always be down,
That will come soon enough,
When I'm cold in the ground.
I choose to be happy; you see
I'm happy, cuz I like me

When you see me and I'm wearing a smile,
Or I say something crazy and act a little wild.
Understand, I'm not looking for accreditation,
Or so insecure that I need validation.
Your acceptance and approval I do not seek.
I am confident and strong by no means weak.
I'm so very happy; you see
I'm happy, cuz I like me

Now, you may see arrogance,
But I'm projecting self-confidence.
This is about me loving myself.
It's not about you, or anyone else.
My reflection in the mirror gives me such glee.
My accomplishments and my failures they complete me.
I'll always be happy; you see
I'm happy, cuz I like me

Life Things

WALK IN MY SHOES

Walk in my shoes,
You'll know my story.
Walk in my shoes,
All my days ain't been in glory.

You'll see the trials and tribulations of my life.
You'll see all the pain and all the strife.
You'll understand my apprehension.
You'll understand the stress and tension.
Understand the reason I keep people at bay,
Because of others I trusted, who went astray.

Walk in my shoes,
You'll know my plight.
Walk in my shoes,
I didn't get here overnight.

You'll see the treachery and lies.
You'll see why I've broken so many ties.
How I've been mistreated.
How I conquered after being defeated.
How I rose above bigotry and hate.
How I've dealt with what is deemed fate.

Walk in my shoes,
And then you'll see,
The foundation which makes me.

WHO DO YOU TURN TO?

Who do you turn to
When the world has turned against you?
Where do you run
When the race is done?
Where can you hide
When all that's left is your pride?

Friends lend a sympathetic ear.
Family encourages you to get in gear.
Enemies find joy in your woe.
There is only one place for you to go.

Retreat to your closet,
Make your deposit.
Fall on your knees,
And enter your pleas.
Ask for guidance and direction,
For comfort and protection.

Turn to the One with ultimate power.
Who's available at any hour.
He'll ease your burdens,
Of this I am certain.

DOING LIFE

I'm doing this thing called Life.
Trying to make it with little or no strife.
The constant drone of the daily grind
Is chipping away at my state of mind.

I'm doing this thing called Life.
Yesterday is already past.
I'm living today as if it's my last.
No guarantee, I'll have tomorrow.
So, I live today without any sorrow.

I'm doing this thing called Life.
Through the struggles,
I must remain strong,
Live it right, so my days will be long.
A constant battle to survive.
A constant will to stay alive.

I'm doing this thing called Life,
A sentence assigned at birth.
Daily, I enrich its worth,
Repaying my obligation,
Expressing my appreciation.

I'm doing this thing called Life.
Revealing my talents and abilities.
Dissolving doubts and insecurities.
Giving the world more,
Than I did the day before.

I'm doing this thing called Life.
Day by day I run,
Knowing the end will come.
This race will be won,
And this thing called Life…
Over and done.

CAUGHT UP

Caught up in this thing called life,
With all the joy there's also strife.
Struggling just to survive,
Hustling just to provide.
The daily grind, so constricting,
Makes living right so conflicting.
The stresses of making ends meet,
Causes some to surrender in defeat.

Caught up in trying to live right,
With no stable conclusion in sight.
The plight of reaching the glass ceiling,
Makes living foul so appealing.
When you're struggling to make a dollar out of fifteen cents,
That three percent increase is no recompense.
No matter how hard you try,
You're still barely getting by.

Caught up in obtaining wealth,
Blind to how it's affecting your health.
Stressing and worrying is taking a toll.
Blood pressure is starting to boil.
Can't get a decent night's sleep,
So fatigue is what your body reaps.
One crisis from a heart attack.
All faculties are out of whack.

Caught up in the art of survival,
You don't see most things are trivial.
So, live your life to all its glory.
Free from stress and worry.
Take time to have some fun.
Because when it's over, it is done.
Nothing will be enough,
And life will end with you, caught up.

UNFORGIVING

It's not so much what you said,
It's what you did.
How you moved to another state and hid,
So you wouldn't have to care of your kid.
Leaving me with all the responsibility,
To provide stability,
To supply a roof, clothes, and food to eat,
To ensure protection and security,
To nurture emotionally,
So your child may function in society.

You chose to run away.
Run the streets and play.
Shirked on your obligation.
Denied your blessed creation.
You missed out on first words and steps.
Lied and made promises that were never kept.
Missed recitals and school plays,
The "Take Your Child to Work" days.
Couldn't be bothered with us at all.
Never picked up the phone to call.

The years have passed on.
The child is now grown.
The streets have turned cold,
Your player's game now old.
Now you want to return
To those that you've burned,
Acting as though you did nothing wrong,
Singing the "I'm Sorry" song.
You've changed your wayward ways,
And will apologize for the rest of your days.

I cannot fathom
Or even imagine
How you could think that I would take you back,
Let you move in or sleep in my sack.
All the struggling I did throughout the years,
Nights I stayed up and wiped away tears,
Struggled to make ends meet,
Kept a roof over our heads and supplied food to eat.
Now you want to return when the hard work is done,
Want to rekindle what we had when we were young.

You can't really think I'm that much of a fool.
I would think that it was cool.

I would fall for that slick charm.
And welcome you back with open arms.
This would be funny, if it wasn't so sad.
But you can never get back what you had.
It's much too little and it's much too late.
And I'm not about to tempt fate.
There will be no reuniting,
Because I'm unforgiving.

THE HAND I WAS DEALT

The hand I was dealt
Was not of riches and wealth.
Money buys many things
Though, sometimes sorrow it brings.
Surrounded in luxury.
Internalized in misery.
Outside seems hunky dory
Inside, it's another story.

The hand I was dealt
Means sometimes I'll struggle.
Fight my way through a concrete jungle.
But, I won't complain.
My mind is sane.
I have health and strength,
Intelligence and common sense.
I can obtain the things I fancy,
But more important the necessities.

The hand I was dealt
Is the hand I play.
Take my life day by day,
Shuffle the cards,
Study long and hard,
Pull from the deck,
Discard those with a negative effect.
Be happy with what I've got.
In reality, I've got a lot.

The hand I was dealt
Is not one of fantasy.
It is my destiny;
Makes me unique,
Makes me complete.
This is His plan.
This is who I am.

SNUBBED BY BETTER

Looking down your nose at me,
Like you're so high and mighty.
Thinking you're so much better than I,
When we both know that's a lie.

You climbed off the backs of others;
Your father, mother, sisters and brothers
Swindled, conned and stole their share.
Flaunted your greed without a care.

You used vile indiscretions
To obtain worldly possessions.
Enemies are plentiful, but friends are few,
Because you think everyone is beneath you.

Everything I gained, I gained on merit.
I did the honorable thing, I worked for it.
Obeyed the law and followed the rules,
Got my education in the best schools.

Treated people with the utmost respect,
Because I know nobody's perfect.
Gave everyone a fair chance,
Didn't step on anyone to advance.

You look at me with disgust.
I look at you with mistrust.
Fast money don't last long.
Karma will right your every wrong.

The problem is you perceive me as a threat.
You're a two-engine plane, I am a jet.
Soaring higher than you will ever get.
You're a long shot, I'm a sure bet.

You're a liar, a robber, and a cheat.
Battling with me will be your defeat.
I will uncover your deceit.
Have you sowing what you reaped.

I'm not on your guest list,
Me, you constantly diss,
I'm so much better than this,
So your silly snubs, I dismiss.

I am world-class supreme.
Self-assured and highly esteemed;
Someone you can only be in your dreams.
Because of the crop, I am the cream!

The pick of the litter,
A real go-getter,
To me, you don't even matter
So, yourself, do not flatter.

Your snobbery is not a fretter
Because
If I haven't been, I will be
Snubbed by better!

YOUR PLAN FOR ME

Your plan
For me....

Please me.
Tease me.
Praise me.
Amaze me.
Thrill me.
Fill me.

Make me.
Take me.
Run me.
Fun me.
Phone me.
Try to
Own me.

Tail me.
Trail me.
Stick me.
Kick me.
Track me.
Act like
You will
Back me.

Bash me.
Slash me.
Pop me.
Drop me.
Dope me.
Take hope.
From me.

Control me.
Mold me.
Defame me.
Tame me.
Despise me.
Tell lies
To me.
Eventually,
You will
Kill Me.

REAL GROWN MEN

Will the real grown men stand up?
The ones who drink from a glass, not a sippy cup,
The ones who don't have a game, they've got a plan.
The ones who know what it means to be a man.

I'm talking about real grown men who:

Don't want a chance with me,
But want to enhance me.
Are not intimidated by my success,
Or view me as just another quest.
Got their priorities in order,
Not trying to be a freeloading boarder.
Don't mind working as a team,
Not destroying my self-esteem.
Will go the extra mile,
To ensure I wear a smile.

You know, real grown men who:

Handle their responsibilities,
Utilize all their capabilities,
Go to work every day,
Struggle to make their own way,
Know chivalry is not dead,
Can keep my mind fed,
Know that relationships take work,
And compromise is the perk,
Know there is no such thing as perfection,
And will ask for directions.

Because real grown men:

Will throw it down,
Hold their ground,
Go downtown,
Without a frown.
Take me to my peak,
Uncover the freak,
Put the lovin' on right,
Hold me all night.
Real grown men,
Know their role
Love me mind, body and soul.

BAGGAGE

What's that you're carrying around?
Has your face wearing a frown
Your self-esteem dragging on the ground
Your soul in the lost and found,
And your heartstrings tightly bound?

You've learned to be discreet
To those in the street
Whom you greet,
Or by chance meet.
They cannot detect your deceit.

Deep down inside,
Is the place you hide,
Tears long cried,
Thoughts of suicide,
Dreams that have died.

You pray to God above,
For that one true love,
That you've dreamt of,
That's pure and fits like a glove.

But it's tough,
Cause, you've got stuff,
Attached with invisible handcuffs,
Which makes relationships rough,
People leave in a huff,
Because they've had enough.

Empty and depleted,
Misused and mistreated,
Abused and cheated,
Damaged and defeated,
A product you created.

Relationships are a task,
Because you're holding on to the past.
Present people put in the cast,
Of a script written too fast,
Of course, relationships won't last.

Your shoulders sag,
Friends think you're a drag.
See you and say "dag",
Here she comes with all those bags.

Of past pains and hurts,
Closet skeletons and dirt.
Do you really want
Baggage as your net worth?

Alone once again,
Seems like in love you just can't win.
When will the cycle end?
This broken heart mend?
Well to begin…
You have to start within.

Don't you understand and know
That in order to grow
To shine and glow
To be free and flow
All that baggage
Has got to go!

CAN'T LET YOU RENT SPACE FOR FREE

Can't let you rent space in my head for free,
I'm saving that space just for me.
Can't deal with your problems and drama,
Don't want to hear about your baby's mama.
You are robbing Peter to pay Paul,
You are ducking the collection man's call.
Your paycheck is spent,
You still gotta make rent.
Everyone has issues with you
Well, I got issues, too.

You never ask about me,
Just want me to see what you see.
How I'm doing is not your priority,
You want me to listen with sincerity.
On and on you go, ranting and raving,
All about the things you are craving.
Things you desire, the love and affection,
But psychotherapy is not my profession.

Want to give me scenarios and ask my advice,
But my conclusions will come with a price.

Listening to all your whining and crying,
My brain's cells are slowly frying.
All the problems you report on,
Are about to cause my fuse shorten.
My brain is full of what I need,
Not for you to come and feed.
I have problems, too,
One, really big one, is you.
Now my nerves are shot,
And I'm about to get HOT!!!

The space in my head is for me,
I keep it free for my sanity.
I don't take in boarders,
Or deal with freeloaders.
I don't live in fear,
My mind is sound and clear.
You keep bringing me nothing but chatter,
Things, to me, that don't really matter.
Go ahead, and let me be,
Cause the space in my head is NOT FOR FREE!!!

KEEPIN' IT REAL

I don't believe in love at 1st sight
Or in the horse ridden by a knight.
Fairy tales are for the young,
Can't put my trust in just anyone.
I treat everyone with a long-handled stick
That way I can't get caught in a trick.
My first instinct is usually true,
Therefore, I'm not surprised by what some do.
Some may say that this is no way to live life,
But this way brings me less strife.
I'm not pessimistic, it's just how I feel,
'Cause I believe in keepin' it real.

If I let my guard down,
I'll end up wearing a frown.
Can't live my life always mad,
Life is too short to be sad.
Keeping everyone at bay,
Will always be my way
But do not despair,
Or worry about my care,
I'm not lonely, I have many friends.
I just don't see them through rose colored lens.
My honesty is really a thrill,
Because they know I'm keepin' it real.

I DON'T WORK ON LAYAWAY

Had a friend, did the date thing and kicked it for a while
Decided to take it to the next level, you know, do the buck wild
Set the mood up with candles and all
Been some time, so I was gonna have a ball
Started the kissin', huggin', and rubbin'
Him tellin' me how I been holdin' out on the lovin'
He starts pushin' my head to go down below
I'm thinkin' he must think that I'm slow
Don't get it twisted
It's just that ladies first is my prerequisite.

So, I tell him fair exchange is no robbery
He just laughs and says I'm so crazy
He says he's never done that before
I'm thinkin', he's about to hit the door
He tells me that he'll do that one day
I freeze and ask, "What did you say?"
He repeats it again.
My head starts to spin.
I put on the brakes.
Oh no, I made a mistake!

One day.
Someday.
Any day.
But not today!!!
I asked him if he saw a layaway sign over my door.
You know, Kmart, Walmart or any other store.
I say I don't work on layaway.

You got to go, you can't stay.
My time is too valuable to play.
Do you remember where the door is?
Let me show you the way.
Cause what you just said constitutes
LAYAWAY!

SNAPPED BACK TO REALITY

It was love at first sight.
I found Mr. Right.
He showered me with love and affection.
Was not bothered by my imperfection.
The words he spoke were so intriguing
Never thought that he was deceiving.

To my dismay
It was all part of his play.
Made me believe he was "The One"
But I was just his fun.
Intuitions detect mistrust
And he's about to leave me in the dust.

But I was smart
Didn't reveal all of my heart
I had some doubts,
So I researched what he was really about.
What I found was something shady
He was broke down, trifling, and sneaky.

My home girl and I rented a car,
Followed him through town, near and far.
He pulled up to another abode
Walked up to a gate and entered a code.
Opened a door and went inside
At that point, all my love died.

Thoughts started running through my head
All the things he said.

All the lies, he spread.
All the things we did in bed.
All the food he was fed.
How astray, I'd been led.

Called him on the phone.
He answered in a hushed tone.
Told him his cover was blown.
I knew where he was and he wasn't alone.
For a second he was thrown.
Then his true colors were shown.

Disheveled, he rushed outside
Adamantly claiming he had nothing to hide.
Beating his chest like King Kong,
Stating he'd done nothing wrong
That I'd flipped the script
Misinterpreted our relationship

That's when the shit hit the fan.
I pulled out a frying pan.
About to deliver a whack.
When my home girl held me back.
I snapped
Back
To reality.
Physical violence, is just not me.

In an instant,
Gained my senses.
He was not worth my time
Or my peace of mind.
He needed to be redefined
Because, I am a rare and precious find.

Naughty Side

BEING BAD

I've tried to be good.
And I would,
If only I could,
Do the things I should,
But, being bad feels so good.

The problem, you see,
Is badness consumes me.
Sends me on a spree,
From which I cannot flee.
Being bad sets me free.

It gives me a sense of power,
Makes me "Queen of the Hour".
Pours out of me like a shower,
Makes goodness cower.
Badness emerges; I am a flower.

Consumption of badness,
Is so easy to digest.
It puts me at my best.
It's in my nature, I guess,
Bad to the bone, I must confess.

I've tried to be good.
And I would,
If only I could,
Do the things that I should,
But being bad feels……
Soooo Damn Good!

MY SECRET OBSESSION

I have a secret to reveal.
It's really not that big of a deal.
Finally admitting how I feel.
Finally realizing it is real.

Judge me if you dare.
What you may think,
I don't care.
This is a full-blown love affair,
Filled with devotion,
Which nowadays is so rare.

This whirlwind romance
Causes my heart to dance,
Allows me to take a chance.
Nightly, I have a standing date
With my ultimate soulmate.
Doesn't matter if I'm early or late,
He'll patiently wait.

His openness is such a comfort.
He's soft, but firm with support.
He misses me when I go away;
And I think about him all day.
Though the alarm clock
May cause me to stray
He's guaranteed to stay
Daydreams of him in my head
Oh, how I love him,
Mr. Bed, Mr. Bed!!!

BEHIND CLOSED DOORS

Behind closed doors,
You got me on all fours.
Begging and squirming for more,
With every entry you hit the high score.
This talent of yours I so adore.
Even if tomorrow, my muscles are sore,
My body's surface is yours to explore.

Behind closed doors, I'll rock your world.
Reveal that I'm a nasty girl,
Suck and lick you, make your toes curl.
Hell, from the chandelier, I'll even twirl,
Make like an oyster and produce a pearl.

Behind closed doors, there's no taboo.
No one will know the things we do.
How the candles emit a psychedelic hue,
How you pull my hair and call me boo,
How I only wear one shoe.
These secrets are shared between us two.

Behind closed doors, we play hide and seek.
Our bodies are how we speak.
Bedsprings and floor boards continually creek.
Tongues and hands explore the cheeks.
Rhythmically grinding to our peaks.
Behind closed doors, we release the freak.

THE LOVE NEST

Scented candles
Adorn the mantle.
Rose petal paths
To a bubble bath.
Where passion meets
Between satin sheets.

Soft jazz
Adds sensuous pizzazz.
A floor and chair dance
Puts a spin on romance.
An exotic lair
Where sex scents the air.

Not a place for the faint-hearted
Inhibitions must be discarded.
A den of exhibitions
All imaginable positions.
Unleashed desires
Inextinguishable fires.

Unplug the phone
In this 'Do Not Disturb' zone.
Hidden away from the outside world
This is where toes are curled.
Insurmountable pleasure
Orgasms beyond measure.

Pornographic sex,
At its best…..
Welcome, to the Love Nest!!!!

UNDER THE COVERS

Under the covers
Where we are uninhibited lovers
The depth of our love is released
All heat of the moment is unleashed
No need for either to speak
Orgasmic satisfaction is what we seek

Our lips meet
Beneath crumbled sheets
Our tongues intertwine
As erotic thoughts race through our minds
Hands explore deep inside my cave
Moans tell you this is what I crave

We twist and turn
Toward the ecstasy we yearn
When I'm with you
Nothing's forbidden or taboo,
The nastier the better,
Is what you say.
The flow of my river,
Proves I like it that way.

Licking and sucking deliciously,
Preparing to take me ravenously.
We begin a rhythmic motion of one.
It continues until we're spent and done.
Our sweat drenched bodies shiver in delight.
As our minds replay the scenes of the night.

Under the covers,
We are uninhibited lovers.
Our freakiness is uncovered.
Erogenous zones and G-spots rediscovered.

IN THE HEAT OF THE FREAK

Can barely unlock the door,
We toss our clothes to the floor.
Your hands are all over me,
Unleashing the tides of my sea.
I tremble at every touch,
Wanting you so much.

Anticipating your every move,
We get into a rhythmic groove.

Sucking and licking sounds reverberate,
We feast off of each other's plate.
Sweat begins to drip,
As we partake on an amorous trip.
Over the vast places,
Of our erotic spaces,
Inhibitions are pushed aside,
Our horniness we can't hide.

My head gets a rush,
With every thrust.
As you excite my sugar walls,
Tears of pleasure fall
Wetness on our cheeks,
Reaching the joy we seek,
Our orgasmic peak,
We can't speak,
In the heat of the freak.

MMM....RIGHT THERE

What a day to be had
Everything that happened was nothing but bad.
Slept through the alarm
Instead of a hot shower, I got warm.

Traffic was heavy on the interstate;
All because I started the day late.
At the office, the project is due,
Figures were right, but the boss found an issue.
Demanded revisions, a whole bunch;
So I didn't eat, had to work through lunch.
Finally made it to the end of the day,
I couldn't wait to get away.

Greeted by you at the door,
A sensual surprise was in store,
Told me to get undressed,
All my tired muscles you would caress.
The rose petals created a path
To a freshly drawn bath.

Washed me and rinsed me off,
Then led me to our bedroom loft.
I lay down on the bed,
You gently massage my neck and head.
You poured and rubbed oil in your hands,
Stress dissolves at your command.

Surreptitiously you move toward the spot.
The place that's guaranteed to make me hot.
Moaning as you get so near;
You lean in and whisper in my ear.
Where?
I say, mmm…right there.

My People, My People

ODE TO CLEO

Standing nearly six foot three,
She was who I wanted to be.
Someone who looks like me, I'd never seen
On TV or on a movie screen.
I was awestruck, joyfully overwhelmed,
By this icon of Blaxploitation film.

Wearing bright Afrocentric clothes
Rocking a perfect afro!!!
Fierce and smooth,
Dominating bad guys with quick karate moves.
Though she could kick ass,
She exuded elegance and class.
Her ride could not be anything less
But a sleek, black Corvette.

As a Federal agent, she worked undercover,
Back home, handsome Bernie Casey was her lover.
In the Black community, they worked in unity,
Treating everyone with respect and dignity.

Ode to Cleopatra,
Not the one of the Nile.
Cleopatra Jones,
A Black Queen of grace and style.

IF IT'S ANY CONSOLATION

Was it a beef between our mothers?
Or you thought I had more than others?
So, when the foreign man came around
You saw a way to profit and get me out of town.
He was looking for people to build a new land.
He would pay you well if you helped with his plan.

You told him about my day,
Showed him the way.
Here I come home walking fast.
Didn't know home would be in the past.
With the trap laid and set,
Out he came with the net,
Threw a hood on me and put me on a boat.
You're about to be paid, so you gloat.

Never gave a second thought to what you did.
You got rid of the uppity kid.
Fantasizing you could live like I was.
But you didn't figure the hidden clause.
You find the foreign man to collect.
He was quick to put you in check.
He said, he's not going to pay you,
Cause, you are going on the boat, too.

We're on the boat, sailing across the sea.
Bound for the new land to work for free.
Instead of getting paid,
You're the foreign man's maid.
Which would be funny, if it wasn't so sad.
Envy had you wanting what I had.

No lesson learned about greed,
You passed it on to your seed.
400 years later and today,
Selling out your own for a big payday.
Blaming the foreign man for your fall.
But, can you blame him for it all?

OUR ANCESTORS ARE CRYING

Our ancestors are crying out from the grave,
Saddened by the way we have behaved.
They were stolen from their land and family.
Taken to a strange land, thrust into slavery,
Their dignity stripped—their pride was a price.
Many gave their lives as the ultimate sacrifice.

Our ancestors are crying out in pain.
Could their struggles have been in vain?
The whippings, rapes, and lynching they endured,
So, their descendants' freedom could be ensured.
Marches and sit-ins were carefully planned,
In order for an equal chance.

Our ancestors are crying out for vengeance,
Yet, we destroy each other in ignorance.
Their trials and tribulations paved the way,
That we, their descendants, could have better days.
Slavery and segregation were some of their plights,
So, we could achieve our civil rights.

Our ancestors are crying out with hurt,
Because we are not showing our true worth.
Descendants of Kings and Queens,
We should excel by any means.
We have no reason to stumble and fall,
For on the shoulders of our ancestors we stand tall.

For all that our ancestors have done,
All the victories in which they've won.
They can rest prouder,
As we have excelled to positions of power.
We can at the very least,
Allow them to rest in peace.
Our ancestors need not cry anymore.
Thanks to them, we now enter through the front door.

Follow Me:

www.authenticallykimartis.com

IG: @authenticallykimartis

Facebook: Authentically Kim Artis

YouTube: authenticallykimartis0525

Emai: authenticallykimartis@gmail.com